ENDURO RACING
ULTIMATE OFF-ROAD TESTS

BY LISA J. AMSTUTZ

CAPSTONE PRESS
a capstone imprint

Published by Capstone Press, an imprint of Capstone
1710 Roe Crest Drive, North Mankato, Minnesota 56003
capstonepub.com

Copyright © 2026 by Capstone. All rights reserved. No part of this publication may be reproduced in whole or in part, or stored in a retrieval system, or transmitted in any form or by any means, electronic, mechanical, photocopying, recording, or otherwise, without written permission of the publisher.

Library of Congress Cataloging-in-Publication Data is available on the Library of Congress website.
ISBN: 9798875226014 (hardcover)
ISBN: 9798875225963 (paperback)
ISBN: 9798875225970 (ebook PDF)

Summary: Zoom! Enduro riders zip through test sections on marked trails. Mile after mile, these brave riders give their all for the win. With carefully leveled, high-energy text, readers will learn about race rules, track features, equipment, and more!

Editorial Credits
Editor: Carrie Sheely; Designer: Dina Her; Media Researcher: Jo Miller; Production Specialist: Tori Abraham

Image Credits
Alamy: Action Plus Sports Images, 16, Kiko Jimenez, 18, Photovision Images/ Stockimo, 4-5, Richard Becker, 7, Robert Grubba, 25, Zoonar GmbH, 21; Getty Images: Alexander Shelegov, 11, Cavan Images, 17, Mustafa Ciftci/Anadolu Agency, 13, 15, 20, 23, Orhan Cicek/Anadolu Agency, 12, 24; Newscom: Jean-Christian Tirat/ SIPA, 29, Panoramic/ZUMAPRESS, 27; Shutterstock: Alexandra Cluj-Napoca, 10, Eugene Onischenko, cover, Weblogiq, 28; Superstock: BlueRed/REDA&CO/Universal Images Group/Universal Images, 8

Design Elements
Shutterstock: backup, Goromaru, JACKREZNOR, Miloje, salam kerrong

Any additional websites and resources referenced in this book are not maintained, authorized, or sponsored by Capstone. All product and company names are trademarks™ or registered® trademarks of their respective holders.

Printed and bound in China. 006276

TABLE OF CONTENTS

All About Enduro 6

Getting Ready 14

Race Time! 20

Going Pro 26

    Glossary 30

    Read More 31

    Internet Sites 31

    Index 32

    About the Author 32

Words in **bold** are in the glossary.

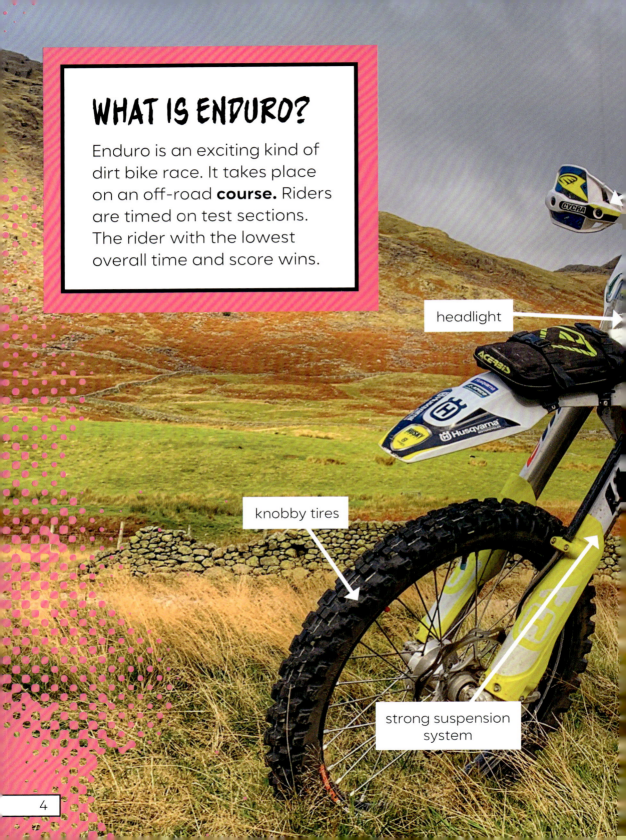

WHAT IS ENDURO?

Enduro is an exciting kind of dirt bike race. It takes place on an off-road **course.** Riders are timed on test sections. The rider with the lowest overall time and score wins.

headlight

knobby tires

strong suspension system

CHAPTER 1
ALL ABOUT ENDURO

Zoom! Dirt bikes roar down the course. They bounce over rocks and logs. They slide on muddy trails.

Almost all enduro races take place outdoors. The courses may run through thick forests or sandy deserts. The **terrain** can be very rugged.

FACT

Events in the SuperEnduro World Championship are held indoors in arenas. The tracks have obstacles such as logs and tires.

An enduro course is long. A race can cover more than 100 miles (161 kilometers). It can last for days! The riders are given breaks. They can refuel their bikes, eat, and make repairs.

Riders go through several test sections, or **stages**. These parts are tricky! They may have steep climbs, rocky trails, or muddy areas. Easier transfer sections are between stages.

There are two main kinds of enduro races. A timekeeping enduro is a race against the clock. Riders try to reach **checkpoints** at just the right time. There is a **penalty** if they are too early or too late.

Restart enduros are similar. But there is only a penalty for arriving to checkpoints late. Riders focus on speed in the test sections.

FACT

There can be secret timed checkpoints. *Shhhh!* Riders don't know where they are.

Hard enduro is just that—hard! The course is **extreme**. What can these riders face? Big logs, boulders, streams, mud pits, and more!

Sometimes events last more than one day. Riders compete for a certain length of time each day.

Enduro bikes must be tough. Riders often add parts. A skid plate helps protect the engine from being damaged by rocks or other objects. A guard protects the chain too.

Enduro bikes travel on- and off-road. They need tires with **tread** that works for both surfaces.

15

It takes skill and strength to compete in enduro. Riders train hard. Some racers train on mountain bikes. This helps them build skills. They practice riding on different types of terrain. Many riders work out too.

FACT
Mountain bikers have enduro races too. These races often have three to six timed stages.

Enduro riders wear a lot of safety gear. It includes a helmet, boots, and goggles. They wear a chest protector and body armor. They also wear pants, a long-sleeved shirt, and gloves.

Before a race, riders check their bikes and gear. They check their **route** sheet too. It shows times, mileage, and turns.

CHAPTER 3
RACE TIME!

It's race time at last! The first group lines up. They're off! The racers zip down the course. They lean in around tight corners.

Riders follow the trail markers. They reach the first test. It's a trail through woods. Each rider twists the throttle. *Zoom!* Trails of dust fly behind the bikes.

FACT

Riders need to watch trail markers. An *X* means caution. A *W* means they're going the wrong way!

The riders go through more tests. Time for a gas stop! The riders fuel up their bikes. Now it's on to the next test. The riders go up a hill with loose, rocky dirt.

24

At last, the racers cross the finish line. Their scores are added. Who will take home the prize?

25

CHAPTER 4
GOING PRO

Professional enduro racing is popular in the U.S. and in Europe. The American Motorcyclist Association (AMA) National Enduro Series is a top event. Pros compete in Enduro World Championship races too.

Pro rider Jane Daniels started riding at age 12. She won the Enduro World Championship four times.

Many other riders compete at top levels. British rider Billy Bolt won his first SuperEnduro World Championship in 2020. He then won three more! In 2024, German rider Manuel Lettenbichler won the tough Romaniacs race for the fifth time.

Manuel Lettenbichler competing in a Romaniacs race

Winners of the 2024 Romanian SuperEnduro race Jonathan Walker (left), Billy Bolt (middle), and Manuel Lettenbichler (right) stand on the podium.

Riders work hard to become pros.

Who will the next superstar be?

GLOSSARY

checkpoint (CHEK-point)—a point along an enduro course where staff mark the time a racer arrives

course (KORS)—a path that racers follow

extreme (ek-STREEM)—relating to a form of a sport that involves an unusually high degree of risk

penalty (PEN-uhl-tee)—something done to give a disadvantage to a competitor, such as points added to an enduro rider's score

route (ROUT)—a plan to get from one place to another

stage (STAYJ)—a section of an enduro race

terrain (tuh-RAYN)—the surface of the land

tread (TRED)—a ridge on a tire that helps it grip the road

READ MORE

Abdo, Kenny. *Motocross.* Minneapolis: Fly!, an imprint of Abdo Zoom, 2024.

Kaiser, Brianna. *Enduro Racing: Rev It Up!* Minneapolis: Lerner Publications, 2023.

Terp, Gail. *Motocross Cycles.* Mankato, MN: Black Rabbit Books, 2024.

INTERNET SITES

American Motorcyclist Association: Enduro
americanmotorcyclist.com/enduro

Fédération Internationale de Motocyclisme: Enduro
fim-moto.com/en/sports/enduro

FIM Hard Enduro World Championship
iridehardenduro.com

INDEX

American Motorcyclist Association (AMA) National Enduro Series, 26

Bolt, Billy, 28, 29

checkpoints, 10, 11

Daniels, Jane, 26

Enduro World Championship, 26, 31

hard enduro, 12

Lettenbichler, Manuel, 28, 29

mountain biking, 16

penalties, 10, 11

refueling, 9, 24

repairs, 9

Romaniacs races, 28

safety gear, 19

SuperEnduro World Championship, 7, 28

timekeeping enduros, 10

tires, 4, 7, 14

trail markers, 22

training, 16

ABOUT THE AUTHOR

Lisa J. Amstutz is the author of more than 150 children's books on topics ranging from applesauce to zebra mussels. An ecologist by training, she enjoys sharing her love of nature with kids. Lisa lives on a small farm with her family.